i don’t care

First published in 2026 by OH
An Imprint of HEADLINE PUBLISHING GROUP LIMITED

1

Disclaimer:
This book has not been licensed, approved, sponsored, or endorsed by Charli XCX

Charli XCX is a registered trademark owned by Charli XCX Inc.

Cataloguing in Publication Data is available from the British Library

ISBN 978-1-03543-652-1

Compiled and written by Malcolm Croft
Editorial: Victoria Denne and Phoebe Hills
Designed and typeset in Avenir by Stephen Cary
Project manager: Russell Porter
Production: Arlene Lestrade
Printed and bound in Dubai

FSC www.fsc.org MIX Paper | Supporting responsible forestry FSC® C104740

Headline's policy is to use papers that are natural, renewable and recyclable products and made from wood grown in well-managed forests and other controlled sources. The logging and manufacturing processes are expected to conform to the environmental regulations of the country of origin.

HEADLINE PUBLISHING GROUP LIMITED
An Hachette UK Company
Carmelite House, 50 Victoria Embankment, London EC4Y 0DZ

The authorised representative in the EEA is Hachette Ireland, 8 Castlecourt Centre, Dublin 15, D15 XTP3, Ireland (email: info@hbgi.ie)

www.headline.co.uk www.hachette.co.uk

i don’t care

THE LITTLE GUIDE TO CHARLI XCX

UNOFFICIAL AND UNAUTHORIZED

CONTENTS

INTRODUCTION – 6

8 CHAPTER ONE — CHARLOTTE'S WEB

38 CHAPTER TWO — BORN TO PLAY

68 CHAPTER THREE — BREAK THE RULES

98
CHAPTER **FOUR**
PARTY GIRL

128
CHAPTER **FIVE**
CULT CLASSIC

158
CHAPTER **SIX**
PURE FUTURISM

INTRODUCTION

For the past decade, Charli XCX has been an unstoppable force in pop music, an outsider too bold to be allowed inside and an artist too big to fit in any one box. Her EDM mixtapes and anthemic club choruses captivated the underground, yet struggled to dominate the mainstream. For years, she was the artist your favourite artists admired, never achieving millions in sales or top awards, but content to dance to her own beat in the margins.

All of this changed, of course, with 2024's colossal hit album, *brat*. Brimming with gritty tunes and IDGAF attitude, it made the entire world mad for more. The record, and its remix, became a cultural phenomenon that, in true brat fashion, they not only defined 2024 but also defiled it – especially when viewed through the lingerie-laced lens of Charli and Billie's knicker-based banger, "Guess".

In a summer filled with incredible new female artistry – from Olivia Rodrigo and Sabrina Carpenter to Chappell Roan – Charli stood out from the crowd by continuing to do what she's always done: remaining unapologtically true to herself. The only thing that changed was that the world finally caught up to her pace.

Though, of course, Charli remains an artist so ahead of the curve that by the time you read this, she'll no doubt have already won her first Academy Award for Best Actress, as predicted, or perhaps even quit music altogether to live in the woods, never to be seen again. With Charli's bold, rebellious spirit, anything is possible – and this unpredictability is precisely what makes her so powerful. Where she goes next… is anyone's guess.

This *Little Guide to Charli XCX* is not merely a collection but a celebration of her most iconic quotes. It draws inspiration from Charli's earliest insights in 2012 right up until today, as she claims her crown as the queen of, well, anything she wants. This tiny tome is packed with Charli's cool-as-fuck charm and original authenticity, making it the perfect pick-me-up for Charli's Angels when they too want to over-indulge their inner brat.

Enjoy!

CHAPTER

ONE

charlotte's web

Welcome to the future of pop music! Inside you'll find all you need to know about how former outsider Charlotte Emma Aitchison transformed into Charli XCX, forcing her way into the mainstream.

It'll never be the same again.

"

I'm a triple threat, which in England means I sing, I drink and I smoke.

"

Charli XCX, her opening monologue as host of *Saturday Night Live*, November 2024

“

To actually come through on the other side – and really feel so connected with my fans through the other side – that was really special.

”

Charli, on the success of her hugely personal 2020 album *How I’m Feeling Now*, which she made in lockdown, interview with Callie Ahlgrim, *Business Insider*, 9 March 2021

"I did a few small acoustic gigs, but I never felt particularly myself, singing on a stage with a guitar. It wasn't until I was 14 or 15 and started going to raves that I felt inspired, performing with my iPod and a mic."

Charli, on ditching the guitar and discovering her true musical style, interview with Jem Aswad, *Variety*, 4 December 2024

“

My parents have always let me have my own space to do what I want to do and be creative.

”

Charli, on her parents, interview with Hannah Mylrea, *NME*, 15 November 2019

"I don't think the fans would be good Charli XCX fans unless they were a bit opinionated, so I'm happy that they've got some spice and sass to them, I suppose."

Charli, on her fans being honest with her, interview with Hannah Ewens, *Rolling Stone*, 2 March 2022

“

I grew up on a diet of Britney Spears and the Spice Girls, and was obsessed with the idea of pop stars. My favourite Spice Girl growing up was Baby. Now, it might be Posh. Looking back at the '90s Spice Girls, it's Posh. She always looked amazing. The little black dress, the strappy shoes, the hair. She looked great. Always.

”

Charli, on her earliest influences, interview with Jessica Goldstein, *Cosmopolitan*, 6 October 2014

"

I feel like I can be six different people in one day sometimes. Which is fun but also really strange in my own brain. I'll surprise myself sometimes with things that come out of my mouth and musically, but maybe that's nice also. But I'm 21. I don't know if people really know who they are until they're dead anyway. You die and you're like: 'I got it! And now I'm dead!'

"

Charli, on Charli, interview with Harriet Gibsone, *The Guardian*, 24 July 2014

> My mum came from a Muslim family where the idea of a 14-year-old going to a rave was completely alien.

Charli, on her mother's heritage, interview with Jeff Weiss, *GQ*, 31 May 2024

"I didn't know anything about rave culture, or club-kid culture, or gay culture – everything was a first that night."

Charli, on her first gig at a club in London when she was 15, interview with Tom Lamont, *The Guardian*, 8 July 2018

“

If I don’t keep a track, it’s because I don’t like it. But I can never tell when something was going to be a hit. *Never.*

”

Charli, on writing for other artists, interview with Kate Mossman, *Observer*, 2 June 2024

"I really just wanted to be Britney Spears when I was younger."

Charli, on her biggest muse, interview with Duncan Cooper, *Fader*, 16 August 2016

“

It was definitely a confusing experience, after ‘Fancy’, when things didn’t really go my way and I didn’t become this huge, big artist or whatever. That was definitely hard for sure.

”

Charli, on the disappointment that came after the success of Iggy Azalea’s 2014 song "Fancy" that she featured on, interview with Tom Lamont, *The Guardian*, 8 July 2018

"Honestly, you can either get on my level and enjoy the fucking party or you can just not be invited because I don't really care, do you know what I mean?"

Charli, on people who don't understand what she's all about, interview with Hannah Ewens, *Rolling Stone*, 2 March 2022

“

I need to find what’s next for me. What is the sound that can’t quite be categorized, you know?

”

Charli, on evolving her sound after popularizing the hyperpop genre, interview with Reanna Cruz, NPR, 18 March 2022

"No matter who you are, sometimes it hurts when people are like, 'You're a fat bitch'."

Charli, on online hate about her appearance, interview with Duncan Cooper, *Fader*, 16 August 2016

Charli wrote her very first song, "Fish and Chips" at the age of 14.

The song's lyrics recount a date she had at a fish and chips shop in London.

In an October 2014 interview with *Billboard*, Charli herself admitted the song was "pretty lame".

Charli's dedicated fanbase, including her 8.5 million+ Instagram followers, affectionately refer to themselves as "Angels".

This moniker is a nod to the popular 2000 blockbuster film *Charlie's Angels*, starring Cameron Diaz, Lucy Liu and Drew Barrymore – a movie that Charli herself has cited as a personal favourite.

The "Angels'"are renowned for their intense loyalty to Charli, who, in turn, embraces her role as the "No. 1 Angel" – a title she also famously used for her third mixtape, released in 2017.

"I had friends, but my school was full of blonde, white girls and I was this half-Indian girl with frizzy hair and different interests. That always made me feel a little bit rejected."

Charli, on feeling like an outsider growing up in the Essex countryside, interview with Jeff Weiss, *GQ*, 31 May 2024

"I wanted my lyrics to be conversational because that's what I think pop culture actually is: it's a 15-second TikTok, a selfie in a cloud, a text to your friends being like 'Where you at, bitch?'"

Charli, on reflecting and creating pop culture in her 2024 album *brat*, interview with Jeff Weiss, *GQ*, 31 May 2024

“

I am extremely proud of my Indian heritage. I love my roots and my family. Don’t call me ‘dirty’ because of the colour of my skin.

”

Charli, on her British-Indian heritage, x.com, February 2016

Charli's first DJ performance was at an illegal warehouse rave in Hackney Wick, East London, UK on 9 August 2007. The event, held in a disused peanut factory, saw Charli perform to approximately 300 people.

Despite her set not being until 3 a.m., 15-year-old Charli arrived early at 9 p.m.! "It was me standing on a speaker with my iPod. I played five songs max," she told *Under the Radar* in March 2025. "People were fucked up, vomiting over each other, and there were so many drugs!" While her mother was "really worried" about the environment, her father "loved it".

Just three weeks after this pivotal performance, Charli celebrated her 16th birthday by signing a major label record deal.

“

I just feel so unbothered by Top 40 success.

”

Charli, on making it in the charts, interview with Tom Lamont, *The Guardian*, 8 July 2018

> "Club electronic music is what makes me feel most alive."

Charli, on club music, interview with Hannah Ewens, *Rolling Stone*, May 2024.

> “For me, the most important thing is that you’re a fucking rock star and your personality is smashing me in the fucking face.”

Charli, on how she decides who she works and collaborates with, interview with Hannah Mylrea, *NME*, 15 November 2019

"I just don't think about my music or my artistry in a two-dimensional way – and I never will."

Charli, on being a three-dimensional artist, interview with Hannah Ewens, *Rolling Stone*, May 2024

“

My dad got offered to buy some MDMA, but he thought that they had said, ‘MDF’, which is a type of wood flooring. So, my dad was like, ‘Well, I don’t have any room in my car at the moment, but give me your number and…’ The dealer was obviously thinking, ‘Wow, this guy must want to buy A LOT of MDMA.’

”

Charli, on her dad at her first major DJ performance at an illegal warehouse rave in 2007, interview with Coleen Nika, *Rolling Stone*, 22 March 2012

> "The first time I fell in love with music was when I was 14, and I was browsing MySpace and I found the Ed Banger Records page."

Charli, on first falling in love with music, interview with Lizzy Goodman, *Elle*, 15 May 2015

"

I always felt like a loser.
I thought if I made music,
people would think I was
interesting. Deep down, one
of my biggest fears was
being boring.

"

Charli, on her inspiration to start making music, interview with Jeff Weiss, *GQ*, 31 May 2024

CHAPTER TWO

born to play

From her Hertfordshire roots to the sun-drenched luxury of her new home in Los Angeles, Charli XCX has remained an unpoppable creative bubble.

Like a sports car, she is perpetually racing forward, and fuelled by her pursuit of innovation, she refuses to slow down or stop, leaving everyone else in her tracks.

Ready to press play?

"In terms of fashion, if you were considered to be doing something wrong in Bishop's Stortford, you were actually probably doing something right."

Charli, on her fashion style as a teenager, interview with Chris Tinkman, *Under the Radar*, 12 September 2013

“

I work really hard and I always stay true to myself and I feel really passionate about what I've done – and the things I've achieved.

”

Charli, on deserving her success, interview with Hannah Ewens, *Rolling Stone*, 2 March 2022

In spring 2023, Charli introduced her creative team to her "Brat Manifesto". This detailed mood board and binder of PDFs was a comprehensive vision for her sixth album.

Breaking from traditional album development, Charli prioritized branding and marketing, meticulously shaping *brat*'s identity before even a single note of music was written. It enabled Charli and her frequent collaborators, including acclaimed producers A.G. Cook and Cirkut, to discern which songs truly aligned with the intended concept. If a track didn't embody "brat" energy, it was discarded.

This innovative and strategic approach laid the groundwork for what would become *the* cultural moment of 2024 – brat summer.

"I see music in colours. I love music that's black, pink, purple or red – but I hate music that's green, yellow or brown."

Charli, on her synaesthesia, interview with Mark Savage, BBC, 12 December 2013

"I'm a workaholic.
To a level that's not cool."

Charli, on how her life is just "partying and making music about partying", interview with Bobby Finger, *Pitchfork*, 6 August 2019

> "My career has been the total opposite of an overnight success story."

Charli, on the widespread success of her 2024 album *brat,* despite already having industry dedication and success for over a decade, interview with Zane Lowe, Apple Music, 8 October 2024

"Wherever I am becomes fun."

Charli, on always being the life of the party, interview with Alex Hawgood, *W Magazine*, 30 January 2025

A.G. [Cook] was like, 'Just call it Charli, because it's you'.

Charli, on her highly personal album *Charli*, interview with Salvatore Maicki, *Fader*, 19 September 2019

"It's become a trend within pop music these days to be very referential of previous hits, which is cool if you're into nostalgia, less cool if you're into pure futurism. I feel like there's a cool middle ground that can be met, which is hopefully what I'm doing."

Charli, referencing the 80s music style of her 2022 album *Crash*, while still being the sound of the future, interview with Hannah Ewens, *Rolling Stone*, 2 March 2022

“

I just fucking like Simon Cowell. He’s very talented at creating celebrity culture and TV shows, and he has an ear as well. I like his vibe and his ambition, and I think I have that. I like the idea of being like a female Simon Cowell.

”

Charli, on meeting Simon Cowell and auditioning to be a guest judge on *X Factor UK*, interview with Duncan Cooper, *Fader*, 16 August 2016

Charli has many famous friends and fans...

"Learning from Charli XCX is like a fucking dream."

Gabbriette Bechtel

interview with Hannah Mylrea, *NME*, 15 November 2019

"Charli is a fucking force."

Matty Healy

interview with Callie Ahlgrim, *Business Insider*, 9 March 2021

"I just want to be around her and be a part of anything she makes."

Troye Sivan

interview with Bobby Finger, *Pitchfork*, 6 August 2019

"I was waiting to be validated by Charli, She is inside the machine and knows how it works and wants to disrupt it."

Héloïse Letissier

interview with Bobby Finger, *Pitchfork*, 6 August 2019

"She's lived and breathed and done everything in the name of pop music for the last 20 years."

Robyn

interview with Shaad D'Souza, *The Face*, 19 February 2024

"*brat* was fucking awesome. Charli's awesome, and she's finally getting the attention that she deserves."

Billie Eilish

interview with Eric Skelton, *Complex*, 5 December 2024

> “I get tired of behaving in a way that people expect me, or expect pop stars, to behave. I’m not a role model – and I never did this because I wanted to be.”

Charli, on being a role model, interview with Shaad D’Souza, *The Face*, 19 February 2024

"The pressures of social media [are] what I find to be quite hard, because it's like a drug. One day the high is really good and the next day you're defeated, it's this constant chase for validation."

Charli, on being so accessible online, interview with Hannah Mylrea, *NME*, 15 November 2019

“

I used to request that my dressing room be trashed, like there'd just been a party in there. It was fun for about two weeks and then we were kind of just sitting in a literal mess.

”

Charli, on her intriguing tour rider requests, BBC Music, 10 August 2022

At just 14 years old, around 2006, Charli began her songwriting journey, crafting her initial tracks on keyboards and acoustic guitar.

By 2008, she uploaded her first collection of songs, a 14-track mixtape simply titled *14* to MySpace. Although never officially released, you can still listen to it on Soundcloud.

Reflecting on this period in a 2016 interview with *Fader*, Charli admitted, "I was rapping about dinosaurs and teddy bears. It was fucking terrible."

“My dream scenario would be getting a plus-10 so I could bring all my best friends.”

Charli, on going to the Grammys with her mates, interview with Alex Hawgood, *W Magazine*, 30 January 2025

"

My two best friends I went to school with, they work for me, we live together. I like to keep business very friend- and family-orientated. Every single thing is work for me. Every friend I have is a collaborator in some way.

"

Charli, on keeping business personal, interview with Tom Lamont, *The Guardian*, 8 July 2018

"I see songwriting for other artists as a creative outlet while I'm creating it, but after the song has been made, I wanna make money. I want the biggest artists to cut these songs, and I want them to be No.1."

Charli, on her "ruthless" attitude when she writes songs for other artists, interview with Duncan Cooper, *Fader*, 16 August 2016

> “I’ll probably never make a record like this again. I’ll probably reject it completely and do something completely different.”

Charli, on not repeating herself, acceptance speech at the BRIT Awards, March 2025

“With *Crash*, I wanted to play into this idea of, ‘What if I played the game?’ It could be deemed a performance art piece, but it’s also a personal test to see whether I can handle it and whether that makes me happy and how it makes me feel.”

Charli, on purposefully succumbing to the pressures and expectations that come with being signed to a major label, and utilising it as a theme for her 2022 album *Crash*, interview with Reanna Cruz, NPR, 18 March 2022

“I think you should spread the hits throughout, you know. One at the beginning, one in the middle and one at the end.”

Charli, on her ideal setlist for her live performances, interview with Michael Cragg, *The Guardian*, 2 June 2015

> There is this misconception that people in the public eye are able to take any shit that you throw at them and yes, we do have to learn how to handle negativity and criticism because it comes with the territory, but at the same time, everyone's a fucking human being.

Charli, on online hate and facing backlash against her 2022 interpolated single "Beg For You", interview with Hannah Ewens, *Rolling Stone*, 2 March 2022

With more than 37 million monthly listeners on Spotify, Charli is one of the most streamed female artists in the world. Incredibly, Charli's combined Spotify streams across all her tracks now exceed 11 billion!

“

I almost just feel like this album title is becoming a self-fulfilling prophecy. I feel very explosive right now. I feel very on the edge, sometimes in a good way, sometimes in a bad way.

”

Charli, on the risk she took with her *Crash* album by straying from her usual style, interview with Hannah Ewens, *Rolling Stone*, 2 March 2022

“

I realized that if I make a party record, I can go on tour and party every night.

”

Charli, on the benefits of making party music, interview with Duncan Cooper, *Fader*, 16 August 2016

At the age of 20, Charli achieved her first major international songwriting success with "I Love It" written for the Swedish pop duo Icona Pop (Caroline Hjelt and Aino Jawo). It exploded onto the global scene in May 2012, and now has more than 1 billion streams on Spotify.

As Charli described to *Glamour* in 2013, "It happened so weirdly and spontaneously. I wrote it in half an hour in my hotel room in Sweden and straight away I knew it wasn't right for me. So, the Icona Pop girls took it and next thing we knew it was becoming a hit everywhere… Surreal."

“

I am a role model for a very flawed, genuinely real, non-perfect person. And that’s all I would ever want to be.

”

Charli, on being a role model, interview with Shaad D’Souza, *The Face*, 19 February 2024

CHAPTER THREE

break the rules

From her non-traditional path to stardom through to her uncompromising, non-conformist vision for her music, Charli XCX's career has been anything but ordinary and boring.

Thank fuck.

If you haven't watched it yet, the 2019 Netflix documentary *I'm With The Band: Nasty Cherry* comes highly recommended. The series chronicles Charli's endeavour to assemble an all-girl punk band named Nasty Cherry, featuring Gabbriette Bechtel on vocals, Chloe Chaidez on guitar, Georgia Somary on bass, and Debbie Knox-Hewson on drums.

The inspiration for the band struck Charli after a particularly wild night out, as she aimed to "form an all-girl group, so I handpicked four incredible women to launch a band in an era of the music industry where there's no roadmap to success." The documentary offers a compelling look at their journey. "I wish when I was 14 there was a band like Nasty Cherry, unashamedly real and badass", Charli claims within.

“

I’m really grateful that Taylor asked me on that tour. But as an artist, it kind of felt like I was getting up on stage and waving to five-year-olds.

”

Charli expressing her opinion about being Taylor Swift’s opening act on Swift’s 2018 *Reputation* tour in an interview with *The Observer*, July 2018

Charli later issued an apology to Taylor Swift and her fanbase, clarifying that “there is absolutely no shade and only love here”

“I want my shows to have this cultish insanity.”

Charli, on her hopes for her live performances, interview with Hannah Mylrea, *NME*, 15 November 2019

> “Dark, magical and cinematic – like a glass of Cherry Coke stained with black lipstick!”

Charli, defining her music in 2011, interview with coldplay.com 2011

> "I've not really sacrificed any part of myself to appeal to more people. It's really rewarding that I've really truly, like, been myself and more people are listening to my music."

Charli, on the unexpected success of her 2024 album *brat*, interview with Zane Lowe, Apple Music, 8 October 2024

16 march 2022

On this day, Charli first shared the concept for her future album with her friends via text message, proposing, "I think it should just be one word on the album cover… Maybe it should be called *brat*."

She later elaborated to *Billboard* in June 2024 that the title became "a jumping-off point for the attitude and brazen ballsiness I want each song to have".

While *brat* undeniably propelled Charli into formidable pop stardom in the summer of 2024, it was her audacious remix album, *brat and it's completely different but also still brat*, released on 11 October 2024, that truly cemented her as an innovator and icon.

This 35-track double album is a masterclass in genre-bending, featuring radical reinterpretations of *brat*'s original tracks featuring a roster of collaborators such as Robyn, Yung Lean, Ariana Grande, The 1975, Troye Sivan, Caroline Polachek, Lorde, Julian Casablancas, Tinashe, Bon Iver, Addison Rae and Billie Eilish.

> “Being a pop icon is very turbulent. The highs are high and the lows are low and the iconic-ness has to stay at such a high level that sometimes you can really get exhausted just from being so, so iconic.”

Charli, on how she presents herself with a fantastical nature, interview with Hannah Ewens, *Rolling Stone*, 2 March 2022

"

It's harder to write really respected party music than it is to write a love song.

"

Charli, on writing rave and electronic music, interview with Duncan Cooper, *Fader*, 16 August 2016

“I’m just so deep in this, I can’t see outside of *brat*, but it’s funny.”

Charli, on how immersive her 2024 album *brat* has become, interview with Kristin Robinson, *Billboard*, 17 July 2024

"Sometimes you're watching your boyfriend's band sell out arena after arena, and that can make me feel small."

Charli, on being in a romantic relationship with The 1975's drummer and songwriter George Daniel, interview with Shaad D'Souza, *The Face*, 19 February 2024

Charli's next few creative projects will focus on her acting, not music.

In the past 18 months, she has completed filming on seven major movies including *The Moment*, *100 Nights of Hero*, *Erupcja*, *Faces of Death*, *I Want Your Sex*, *Sacrifice* and *The Gallerist*. Which one will you see first?

“I’m in a space that only I could be in. Nobody can do what I do, apart from me.”

Charli, on being unique, interview with Tom Lamont, *The Guardian*, 8 July 2018

“

It could be cool if I didn’t really make music anymore after *brat*. I’m definitely thinking about it because I really want to act.

”

Charli, on her desire to act, interview with Kristin Robinson, *Billboard*, 17 July 2024

“Obviously I’m going to deliver something iconic. Don’t doubt me.”

Charli, on her fans suspicion of the concept of her album *Crash*, interview with Justin Curto, *Vulture*, 22 March 2022

"I like what I like. I'm not ever thinking about – especially recently – the success of something. And that was very true for *brat*. I wasn't thinking that it would be very successful at all, despite believing in the music massively. I was making it for myself. To please everybody is pointless."

Charli, on *brat* and its success, interview with Alex Hawgood, 30 January 2025

> "I've definitely become more of a bitch. I'm having more diva tantrums."

Charli, on her persona while creating *brat*, interview with Jeff Weiss, *GQ*, 31 May 2024

“

What’s life without a bit of trouble?

”

Charli, on sometimes being called out for things she says, interview with Bella Spratley, *Metal Magazine*, 21 February 2020

> “When you’re a big artist, you can choose when you want to be around other artists with big egos.”

Charli, on her associations with other famous artists, interview with Shaad D’Souza, *The Face*, 19 February 2024

How 2 Live Ur Life the XCX Way

1. Party hard

2. Treat others how you would like to be treated (I know it's cheesy but it's cool to be kind!!!!)

3. Love the gays!! They started everything!!

4. Voice ur opinion

5. Listen to Charli XCX songs every day. This is v. important.

Charli's five rules for "How 2 Live Ur Life the XCX Way", as she proclaimed in December 2018 for *Coup de Main*

“

The whole idea of being a brat is interesting to me, because why are people brats? Why do people act out and be difficult and misbehave? I think it's because sometimes you're overcompensating for insecurity or feeling uncomfortable, and I think that's where the two fit together.

”

Charli, on the concept of brat, interview with Cynthia Littleton, *Variety*, 7 December 2024

"When I got signed, I wanted to make bad rap music. I didn't know who I was. I didn't know what I liked. Even though I was signed, I was still figuring it out."

Charli, on her earliest music, interview with Kate Hutchinson, *The Guardian*, 30 November 2013

“I like driving, and that’s obviously a big part of L.A. too. It’s kind of a perfect city for me.”

Charli, on living in Los Angeles, interview with Dan Adler, *Vanity Fair*, 17 September 2019

“

With *brat*, it was really interesting to just do things for the fan base and make that feel exclusive – but then once you’re in the club, it’s actually very inclusive.

”

Charli, on the themes of inclusivity and exclusivity in her 2024 album *brat*, interview with Kristin Robinson, *Billboard*, 17 July 2024

“For those of you who recognize me, you might know me from my album *brat*, but don’t worry if you don’t; there is nothing wrong with being straight.”

Charli, making a joke about her only appealing to the gay community, *Saturday Night Live* opening monologue, November 2024

> “The more I’ve grown up and the more I’ve become secure with myself, I’ve become comfortable with being questioned.”

Charli, on becoming more secure in herself and her identity, interview with Duncan Cooper, *Fader*, 16 August 2016

“There is a misconception that I’m just this person who parties every single day and is really confident and loud and gets drunk all the time. And that’s part of it, but also I’m a business woman, and I can be really shy sometimes.”

Charli, on being a multifaceted individual despite her reputation, interview with Hannah Mylrea, *NME*, 15 November 2019

“The main relationship in my life is the one I have with the industry I’m in, and the way it makes me feel. Sometimes it makes me feel incredible and sometimes it makes me feel like nothing.”

Charli, on her relationship with the music industry, interview with Shaad D’Souza, *The Face*, 19 February 2024

CHAPTER FOUR

party girl

Charli XCX is a true 365 party girl, devoted to having a good time all the time – and dedicated to sucking the seriousness out of pop music and blowing the fun back in.

In fact, Charli's so committed to the party, she's made it not only her lifestyle, but artistic vision and career.

Let's party!

> The times you let go and feel some kind of euphoria or a sense of super happiness is often, for me, at a party. I think partying is an important part of growing up.

Charli, on the quintessential collaboration between "art and partying", interview with Emma Garland, *Vice*, 17 November 17 2017

> "I kinda miss the time where pop music was really volatile and crazy. I miss the Paris Hilton days! Everybody is so worried about everything right now, how they're perceived, if this art they've created is going to offend."

Charli, on hyper-perception, especially as an artist and public figure, interview with Shaad D'Souza, *The Face*, 19 February 2024

“I didn’t want any metaphors – like, at all. I wanted this record to feel like I was having a conversation with the listener in a true way. I could say that to you in the back of a cab on the way to a club.”

Charli, on songwriting for her 2024 album *brat*, interview with Kristin Robinson, *Billboard*, 17 July 2024

"

I really care about being an artist who has a vision, is unique and not a carbon copy of anybody else. I also like other artists who create their own world, and it feels like nobody else could do it like them.

"

Charli, on being original, interview with Aaliyah Harry, *Grazia*, 11 November 2021

The success of the *brat* album in summer 2024 transcended music, sparking a cultural movement. "brat summer" profoundly influenced fashion, social media and even politics, and the word "brat"* was officially named *Collins Dictionary*'s "Word of the Year" for 2024.

The dictionary redefined it as describing someone possessing a "confident, independent and hedonistic attitude".

* The word "brat" dates back to the early 1500s. Its original usage was to describe the child of a beggar, deriving from the Celtic word "bratt", meaning "cloak" – the common attire of beggars.

> "The reason people relate to *brat* is because people want to be a little bit messy and own the imperfect parts of themselves."

Charli XCX, on why *brat* resonated so much with listeners, interview with Kristin Robinson, *Billboard*, 17 July 2024

"I believe I deserve this. I believe I deserve everything that could maybe happen. And I don't think that's a cocky thing to say because I've worked really hard and I've never bitten the hand that fed me and I've always been really respectful."

Charli, on deserving her success, interview with Harriet Gibsone, *The Guardian*, 24 July 2014

“I don’t really take industry advice or influence at all and I think that’s how I’ve got to where I am. I think anybody that claims to know what is right for you creatively, especially in the music that you make, is just an idiot. I just don’t trust anybody’s advice when it comes to my own music.”

Charli, on only trusting herself with her music, interview with Bella Spratley, *Metal Magazine*, 21 February 2020

“

I’m like, ‘Fuck! I’m a fucking popstar.’

”

Charli, on how it feels to perform to an audience chanting her name, interview with Hannah Mylrea, *NME*, 15 November 2019

“Desire is cultivated by being a little bit hard to reach, a little bit separate.”

Charli, in reference to the marketing of pop music, interview with Kristin Robinson, *Billboard*, 17 July 2024

> “My gut instinct has got me this far.”

Charli, on trusting herself, interview with Reanna Cruz, NPR, 18 March 2022

> “I don’t have anyone I can talk to about not-music stuff. Everything is music.”

Charli, on being a "workaholic", interview with Tom Lamont, *The Guardian*, 8 July 2018

Charli's sheer, bra-less Dilara Findikoglu gown at the March 2025 BRIT Awards, revealing her nipples, sparked 825 Ofcom complaints.

The striking Goth-inspired dress caused a "furore" with broadcaster ITV.

True to form, Charli addressed the "scandal" directly during her acceptance speech: "I heard that ITV were complaining about my nipples. I feel like we're in the era of 'free the nipple' though, right?"

> “That’s why they are my fans: they like my drama, my bitchiness, my stubbornness, my life, whatever. They do!”

Charli, on the dedication of and connection to her fans, interview with Reanna Cruz, NPR, 18 March 2022

> “The idea behind the ‘Boys’ music video is to revert the male gaze in pop videos. But also just to make a really fun pop video with everyone’s favourite dudes!”

Charli, on her music video for her 2017 single "Boys", which now has more than 200 million YouTube views, and stars Joe Jonas, Charlie Puth, Stormzy, Mark Ronson, Jack Antonoff, Tom Daley and will.i.am, interview with Emma Garland, *Vice*, 17 November 2017

“

I hate it when musicians dive into a different field, head-first, without... researching or learning much of anything about it. I did a lot of reading to educate myself about acting over the past three years before I actually did anything.

”

Charli, on her burgeoning acting career, interview with Jem Aswad, *Variety*, 4 December 2024

“

I made my artist name "Charli XCX" up when I was 15 years old. It was the first time I had to play a rave, and the guy asked me what I wanted to put on the flyer. I can't just put my normal name, because that's pretty crap.'

”

Charli, on the origins of her artist name, interview with Lauren Nostro, Complex, 6 March 2013

XCX

Charli began using the suffix "XCX" when she was only eight years old, while a pupil at Herefordshire's prestigious Bishop's Stortford College.

She would sign off from chats with friends on MSN Messenger, an early online chat platform, "Charli xcx".

"XCX" simply stood for Kiss Charli Kiss.

"Matty Healy is like my brother now. I have endless amounts of respect for him as a songwriter and him as a person but I sometimes want to strangle him."

Charli, on working and collaborating with the often-controversial lead singer of The 1975, Matty Healy, interview with Zane Lowe, Apple Music, 8 October 2024

“There’s nothing I hate more than being put in a box. So really, my main drive was to do the opposite of what people expected from me.”

Charli, on breaking expectations and audience perceptions and predictions, interview with Sasha Geffen, *Crack Magazine*, 18 November 2021

“I’m beginning to feel like the people who know, know. And the people who don’t? They wouldn’t get it anyway.”

Charli, on her fans and her critics “getting” her music and vibe, interview with Bobby Finger, *Pitchfork*, 6 August 2019

“

My dad always encouraged me to be weird. He always said that following fashions, trends and the crowd was such a terrible trait.

”

Charli, on her dad’s philosophy to life, interview with Chris Tinkham, *Under the Radar*, 12 September 2013

During 2024, many pondered: what exactly is "brat"?

Charli explained its essence to the BBC in November 2024: "it's an attitude, it's a vibe." She described "keeping it real" as very "brat," along with being "honest, blunt and a little bit volatile."

For those looking to embrace their inner "brat", Charli also offered a simple checklist:

- A pack of cigarettes
- A Bic lighter
- A Strappy white top with no bra

“

I don’t listen to a lot of other music aside from people that I work with or my own, which probably sounds really narcissistic and crazy. But I work with people because I think they’re the best.

”

Charli, on her love for her collaborators, interview with Christopher Rosa, *Glamour*, 13 September 2019

> “I’ve always felt like an outsider, particularly in the British music industry. So it feels really nice to be recognised on this album, when I haven’t made any sacrifices.”

Charli, on being an outsider, BRIT Awards acceptance speech, March 2025

"I'm living proof that maybe it takes a long time, but you don't need to compromise. You don't need to compromise your vision. It's kind of the long road, but if you do your own thing and you do it well, eventually, I think if you believe in yourself enough, and honestly, if you make good enough music, people will resonate with you and be right there with you."

Charli, on never compromising her vision, BRIT Awards acceptance speech, March 2025

"The reason I love electronic music and clubs and DJs so much is that everything is endless. Everything can be repurposed, reimagined."

Charli, on the endless creativity of club and electronic music, interview with Kristin Robinson, *Billboard*, 17 July 2024

> I feel like I've earned the right to do whatever the fuck I want because I'm good enough. I'm better than a lot of people.

Charli, on making her own decisions and using her best judgement, interview with Sasha Geffen, *Crack Magazine*, 18 November 2021

CHAPTER FIVE

cult classic

Charli XCX is the walking, talking definition of a cult classic: an artist independent enough to feel utterly real, yet undeniably influential enough to endure and reshape the sound of pop for others to follow...

“

I actually see *Pop 2* as one of my most important bodies of work, as I think my fans do too.

”

Charli, on *Pop 2*, her monumentally popular 2017 mixtape, interview with Salvatore Maicki, *Fader*, 19 September 2019

> “I’m Charli XCX. I make music for myself, not for anybody else.”

Charli, on being loyal to her sound over audience expectations, interview with Reanna Cruz, NPR, 18 March 2022

The cover art for Charli XCX's *brat* album has become as iconic as the music itself.

Charli intentionally chose the "actually quite disgusting" toxic-slime green colour, specifically Pantone 3570-C, for its unsettling effect.

She aimed to give her fans "something not very pretty", challenging them to "look at yourself and wonder why it bothers you so much that my face isn't on the cover?"

"We knew it was going to be green, but the conversations around the shade of green were weeks long."

Charli, on the meticulous attention to detail for the album cover and marketing for *brat*, interview with Kristin Robinson, *Billboard*, 17 July 2024

> I really like pop music, but I've always really liked being a freak too!

Charli, on having a "hybrid artist identity", interview with Bella Spratley, *Metal Magazine*, 21 February 2020

“

Sometimes I don’t understand why I’m not bigger than I am.

”

Charli, on her "authenticity" holding her back from mainstream success, interview with Bobby Finger, *Pitchfork*, 6 August 2019

“

By the time the mainstream cares about what I’m doing right now I’ll have moved on to the next three things. I am ahead of the game.

”

Charli, on creating music trends, not simply following them, interview with Bella Spratley, *Metal Magazine*, 21 February 2020

“Now every single move I make is considered in depth. I think about every element of my artistry so in depth that I feel truly potent now.”

Charli, on being intentional, interview with Kristin Robinson, *Billboard*, 17 July 2024

"

I just want people to listen to my record and either smile if they want to or cry if they want to. That's what I would love to happen to people. And if you were to come and see me live, I would just want them to be completely free and open and lose their minds and go crazy.

"

Charli, on how she wants her fans to feel, interview with Dale Eisinger, *Consequence*, 18 April 2013

"

Everything is lost when I'm onstage. It's just me and the microphone and the music and me going crazy and losing myself. I don't think. I don't plan. I just do. And that's often why I do a lot of embarrassing things, like terrible dancing and flashing my pants. I don't care. I'm not thinking about it. I don't give a fuck about that shit or what people say.

"

Charli, on her live performances, interview with Chris Tinkham, *Under the Radar*, 12 September 2013

"Matty Healy suggested to George that maybe I had a crush. We do the same thing, we understand the same world, we challenge each other. I think George is really hot and funny. I feel inspired to be with someone who's unbelievably talented. That's really sexy to me."

Charli, on her now-husband, George Daniel, of the rock group The 1975, interview with Shaad D'Souza, *The Face*, 19 February 2024

“Charli’s conviction, honesty and vulnerability are the most potent things that make her a brilliant artist and songwriter. You believe absolutely everything she does.”

Husband George Daniel, on Charli, interview with Jem Aswad, *Variety*, 4 December 2024

"I do naturally gravitate toward the queer community. I just feel that energy supporting me so much. I really wouldn't be where I am without that community. When we go out, it's often with the community at an LGBTQ+ club or night or something like that. Everyone has better taste in the queer community, anyway."

Charli, on her majority LGBTQ+ audience, interview with Christopher Rosa, *Glamour*, 13 September 2019

“

Being an artist, you always know that your work means something to the people who communicate with you or show up at your shows. But during lockdown, I really did realize, 'Wow, my songs can really help shift somebody's mood'.

”

Charli, on having purpose and feeling more connected with her fans during lockdown, interview with Sasha Geffen, *Crack Magazine*, 18 November 2021

On 22 February 2024, Charli delivered a hyper-viral three-hour, 29-song Boiler Room rave at a warehouse in Bushwick, Brooklyn, New York.

Donning her now-iconic blue T-shirt emblazoned with "CULT CLASSIC", she performed for just 400 extra-lucky fans from a rumoured 25,000 applicants. The "PARTYGIRL" set, dubbed "a cultural reset", featured Charli DJing remixes of her own discography alongside covers.

In *Rolling Stone* (May 2024), she confessed, "I was so fucking nervous! Looking back at some of the footage when we were doing the edit, I literally look terrified. I haven't DJ'd with eight cameras in front of my face before."

> “It feels like underground scenes are back and people just want to be in physical spaces and be a part of something.”

Charli, on the praise of her 2024 Boiler Room set, interview with Jeff Weiss, *GQ*, 31 May 2024

“

I don’t really sleep these days. Um, what year is it? 2024 has not been a very restful year, for sure.

”

Charli, on the Year of Charli XCX, interview with Jem Aswad, *Variety*, 4 December 2024

“

Before *brat* came out, I was saying to everyone around me, ‘Be prepared that this is probably going to be the album that doesn’t perform very well at all.’ Because I was like, ‘I’m just going to make songs about my friends. I’m going to name check them all.’ I don’t really care if anybody else likes it. I just need to do this because the previous record was so about me trying to appeal.

”

Charli, on *brat*, interview with Eli Russell Linnetz, i-D.com, 4 September 2024

“I feel like I am one of the few artists who has a foothold in both the mainstream Top 40 world and the more left-of-centre underground world.”

Charli, on her uniqueness as a mainstream and underground artist, interview with Bobby Finger, *Pitchfork*, 6 August 2019

“

Make time for the things that you love.

”

Charli, giving life advice, interview with Jem Aswad, *Variety*, 4 December 2024

Charli has many famous friends and fans...

"I've been blown away by Charli's melodic sensibilities since 2011. Her writing is surreal and inventive, always."

Taylor Swift

New York Magazine, August 2024

"I love her so much. She's worked her arse off, and it's so beautiful to see her get the recognition she deserves."

Dua Lipa

Billboard, December 2024

"She is in her prime right now; she works so hard, and she is a super mega-big pop star."

Katy Perry

Pinkvilla, July 2024

"Charli has been able to bridge the gap between leftfield, avant-garde electronic music and indulgent, satisfying, clean pop, and it's just the coolest shit in the world."

Izzy Camina

Red Bull, October 2020

"Charli has been not only a great mentor for me but also a big sister, in a way – the coolest, sickest, nicest, most fun sister you could ever have. I'm one of her biggest fans. It's truly a gift from God."

Addison Rae

interview with Shaad D'Souza, *The Face*, February 2024

"Lovely but fearless."

Rina Sawayam

interview with Hannah Ewens, *Rolling Stone*, March 2022

"My fans really care about me, and I really care about them. We're speaking the same language, and maybe nobody else gets that language, but we totally understand. I just feel my music is now a safe space for me to be really honest. I don't feel afraid."

Charli, on her fans, interview with Christopher Rosa, *Glamour*, 13 September 2019

“

We live in a world where we are so focused on our own consumption and our outward presence to the world – what people think of us, the way we are perceived – that sometimes it's very hard to be in the moment. I definitely struggle with that.

”

Charli, on the struggle to be present, interview with Bella Spratley, *Metal Magazine*, 21 February 2020

“More than ever now, people are rewarding the niche. Finally, it seems fine that I'm just myself, and suddenly people like it. It's good to finally be accepted. I'm happy with the winding path I've taken, and with my status as more of an outsider, because sometimes I feel a bit awkward being in the club. I'm at peace with it all. It's all cool.”

Charli, on being niche and an outsider, interview with Kate Mossman, *Observer*, 2 June 2024

“

Am I a leftfield underground artist or am I a pop star? I’ve always been caught in this dichotomy.

”

Charli, on her identity in the music industry versus what she wants to represent, interview with Zane Lowe, Apple Music, 8 October 2024

> For me, being a true artist with global impact is much more than just having a good voice or a big song or a good album, it's about having a personal identity, which can sometimes be volatile. It can't be tamed. It can't be squeezed neatly into an easily defined box and it can never ever, really, truly be replicated.

Charli, on her global impact, ASCAP Global Impact Award ceremony, Los Angeles, 8 May 2024

“

A good artist constantly evolves and challenges their audience, because they know their audience is smart enough to be challenged.

”

Charli, on what it means to be a good artist, x.com, May 2021

CHAPTER SIX

pure futurism

The world of tomorrow sounds like the music Charli XCX is making today; her songs are the soundtrack of the next generation, as is her approach to how she sells herself to the world, from marketing her "brat manifesto" to her bold career choices.

All of it is pure futurism…

> “I’m really into dumb, hook-y choruses. That’s my favourite thing about pop music, when a song is so dumb that it’s clever.”

Charli, on what makes a good pop song, interview with Jeff Weiss, *GQ*, 31 May 2024

> “If I go on holiday for three days, I have a breakdown. That’s when everything around me is still, and I have time to question everything I’ve done.”

Charli, on processing things when she actually takes a break, interview with Bobby Finger, *Pitchfork*, 6 August 2019

“If I was a man, I would be more accepted for what I’ve done.”

Charli, on gender inequality in mainstream music events and productions, interview with Andrew Trendell, *NME*, 13 February 2020

“

I respect my fans so much. I wouldn’t be the artist that I am without them. They saved me, you know? When I was lost, they showed me who I could be.

”

Charli, on her fans inspiring her to become her best self, interview with Sasha Geffen, *Crack Magazine*, 18 November 2021

"From my music to everything I've done in my career, it's always been about following my own path and doing things a bit differently."

Charli, on not following the "status quo", interview with Aaliyah Harry, *Grazia*, 11 November 2021

“

I’m too British for therapy.

”

Charli, on perhaps needing therapy – but not going!, interview with Emma Garland, *Vice*, 17 November 2017

“

Clubs are really fruitful, creative spaces for me. I get inspired lyrically, visually, the whole thing. The light and lasers in clubs or at raves, the space itself. It's very inspiring to me.

”

Charli, on being inspired by clubs, raves and partying, interview with Christopher Rosa, *Glamour*, 13 September 2019

“

The club can be a church for somebody. It’s like a community of people who are just letting go and being free. It’s like gay church.

”

Charli, on dancing in clubs being a spiritual experience, interview with Christopher Rosa, *Glamour*, 13 September 2019

“

My best ideas always just come when I’m at a microphone singing nonsense. And afterward, when I figure out a melody, I put lyrics to it. Or maybe I’ll have written some lyrics on my phone and a song will start from that. I don’t really have a process. It’s always messy.

”

Charli, on her songwriting process, interview with Jessica Goldstein, *Cosmopolitan*, 6 October 2014

“

I struggled performing for a while to the crowds who were more music lovers, rather than people who wanted to take drugs, party and listen to DJs. I’ve always been trying to get back to that party energy.

”

Charli, on her ideal audience, interview with Jeff Weiss, *GQ*, 31 May 2024

“I have full freedom of speech as an artist. It’s pretty cool, I’m on a major label but I operate like an artist who isn’t and that’s really exciting for me because I’m kind of left to do what I want.”

Charli, on having boundless creativity despite being signed to Atlantic Records, interview with Bella Spratley, *Metal Magazine*, 21 February 2020

“

When you’re 21, you can go full throttle: fucking party, drink, be an idiot, and still feel fine. You can go to shoots kind of drunk, but not really show it. You can do it all.

”

Charli, on how she was able to keep going despite the high pressure and constant travelling, interview with Jeff Weiss, *GQ*, 31 May 2024

“

Stripper heel over a comfortable slip-on – any day.

”

Charli, on her preferred performance footwear, interview with Michael Cragg, *The Guardian*, 2 June 2015

"I'm a pessimist in a big way. I'm never happy with what I've done."

Charli, on how she never feels totally satisfied professionally, interview with Emma Garland, *Vice*, 17 November 2017

"Real life is fucked up. Real life is a mess. No one looks perfect. No one is perfect – and that's great."

Charli, on the inauthenticity of social media content, interview with Bella Spratley, *Metal Magazine*, 21 February 2020

"

I have no interest in working with someone just because they're the new hot shit. I have interest in working with people who inspire me and people I think could make an impact on pop culture and the way music sounds.

"

Charli, on who inspires her and how she decides who to collaborate with, interview with Emma Garland, *Vice*, 17 November 2017

On 19th July 2025,
Charli married her partner,
The 1975 drummer George
Daniel, at Hackney Town Hall
in London.

She tied the knot wearing a
classic Vivienne Westwood
bridal gown accompanied by
her signature black sunglasses,
and of course, the big day had
to finish with a late-night rave
in edgy East London… she
has her party girl reputation to
maintain after all.

This was followed by a second wedding celebration in Sicily, Italy, two months after formally saying "I do".

The event was a star-studded affair, with the guestlist including George's bandmates, as well as Troye Sivan, Julia Fox, Robyn, Amelia Dimoldenberg and many of Charli's other famous friends.

"I'm constantly going back and forth in my conflict around fame and what constitutes success. This new music of mine is not going to be played in Starbucks. It's pop music but I'm being true to myself. But I also know that if I chose a slightly different, maybe more palatable path, I do have the skills as a songwriter to write big Top 40 pop hits."

Charli, referencing her multi-talented abilities and choosing to focus on what she wants to create, no matter the outcome, interview with Jeff Weiss, *GQ*, 31 May 2024

“

So much stuff happens at parties. You meet people who you fall in love with You’re with some of your best friends. You break up with someone. It’s this huge social concoction of all of these people that you know and don’t know. Partying is a place where I feel very free. Partying always means more than just a party.

”

Charli, on her music being inspired by clubs, raves and partying, interview with Christopher Rosa, *Glamour*, 13 September 2019

> “There’s been quite a lot of tension between the way I’ve chosen to do things and the way a major label expects female pop artists to do things.”

Charli, on not rejecting a traditional female artist trajectory while being signed to a major label, interview with Reanna Cruz, NPR, 18 March 2022

"My favourite ritual when it comes to self-care is getting out of the city that I'm in and going into nature. The sound of nature feels very grounding."

Charli, on her self-care rituals, interview with Bella Spratley, *Metal Magazine*, 21 February 2020

“

Crash plays into the idea of what a stereotypical pop star is often deemed to be and looking at the boxes women are often put in – the virgin, the whore or the vixen – and kind of exploring what those themes are within pop music, and the way that the music industry can sometimes perceive women and characterize them. For *Crash*, I was exploring the idea of what the most sexualized, heightened, vampiric version of myself could be.

”

Charli, on the themes of her 2022 album, *Crash*, interview with Reanna Cruz, NPR, 18 March 2022

"

Music affects me so much more emotionally when I hear it at a party and I'm a bit fucked up rather than listening to it at home.

"

Charli, on the collaboration between "art and partying", interview with Emma Garland, *Vice*, 17 November 2017

“

I’ve heard people say to me, ‘How can you claim to be a feminist when you dress like that?’ I’m not a dumb idiot just because of what I wear.

”

Charli, on feminism, interview with Jessica Goldstein, *Cosmopolitan*, 6 October 2014

“It’s almost a necessity for the validity of an artist for them to be considered real or genuine or down to earth. All this stuff feels very sort of Bob Dylan to me, which I don’t really care about personally. I love selling out. Pop is supposed to be a fantasy, right?”

Charli, on selling out, interview with Reanna Cruz, NPR, 18 March 2022

“I think the *brat* campaign is so good because we’re so fucking bullish and laser-focused on every single fucking thing.”

Charli, on the meticulousness of the marketing for her 2024 album *brat*, interview with Jeff Weiss, *GQ*, 31 May 2024

> “We’re in this disposable culture now more than ever – and I’m here for it.”

Charli, on the current cultural climate, interview with Reanna Cruz, NPR, 18 March 2022

“Now that hyperpop has become a genre where people can bracket a lot of artists with familiar sounds in one group, it feels less exciting to me to play within that space.”

Charli, on evolving her sound after popularizing hyperpop, interview with Reanna Cruz, NPR, 18 March 2022

“

When I make my music, I’m looking to fulfil a very selfish need to just make what I want to hear. I really just want to make songs that I want to hear in the club, and I want to make them in a very spontaneous way.

”

Charli, on what she wants out of the music she makes, interview with Dan Adlery, *Vanity Fair*, 18 March 2022

“That’s what the essence of ‘brat’ is – tapping into that part of yourself that only you can access. It’s ignoring the things that make your palatable or comparable to others.”

Charli, on her definition on the essence of brat-ness, interview with Zane Lowe, Apple Music, 8 October 2024.

“

The aim of my music is to make people feel confident and free – I just want everyone to feel hot!

”

Charli, on the intention behind her music, interview with Aaliyah Harry, *Grazia*, 11 November 2021

"I'm gonna be around for a really long time, whether I have number ones or not. Maybe I won't always be an artist. Maybe I'll be a songwriter. But I will have changed the landscape of what pop music is. I already have. I really believe that. I know it sounds really arrogant to look you in the eyes and say it, but I have."

Charli, on her impact on pop music – so far!, interview with the *Evening Standard*, 20 September 2019